# TABLE OF CONTENTS

# NOTE

Scripture quotations are from the American Standard Version of the Bible (1901), unless otherwise indicated.

# I JOHN

## SEEING CHRIST IN CHRISTIAN FELLOWSHIP

*That which was from the beginning, that which we have heard, which we have seen with our eyes; that which we contemplated, and our hands handled, concerning the word of life; (and the life has been manifested, and we have seen, and bear witness, and report to you the eternal life, which was with the Father, and has been manifested to us:) that which we have seen and heard we report to you, that ye also may have fellowship with us; and our fellowship is indeed with the Father, and with his Son Jesus Christ. And these things write we to you that your joy may be full. And this is the message which we have heard from him, and declare to you, that God is light, and in him is no darkness at all. If we say that we have fellowship with him, and walk in darkness, we lie, and do not practise the truth. But if we walk in the light as he is in the light, we have fellowship with one another and the blood of Jesus Christ his Son cleanses us from all sin.*

*I John 1:1-7*

*Let us pray:*

Dear heavenly Father, we have read Thy word and now we ask that Thy Holy Spirit will open Thy word to our hearts that we may hear Thy voice, that we may be drawn into Thy fellowship, that Thy name may be glorified. So, we just commit this time into Thy hands and ask Thee to do the work that Thou dost want to do. In the name of our Lord Jesus. Amen.

The apostle John wrote three letters-those which are known as the first, second and third letters of John. Chronologically speaking, these are the very last writings of the New Testament, since he wrote these letters after he had written the Gospel according to John and the book of Revelation. John's first letter is addressed to no particular church, the second and third letters are addressed to individuals. However, when we read these three letters we can very easily discern that all three have something in common-they all are dealing with one essential issue: fellowship.

This first letter of John is rather unusual. Normally, a letter will have a beginning address, a salutation, and a closing greeting or remark. But in this letter there is neither a beginning nor an ending in the formal sense of a letter; nonetheless, there is no mistaking that this writing is in the form of a letter because throughout there is such a personal, intimate atmosphere and tone about it.

This letter was probably written between the years 95 and 98 A.D. by the apostle John. Of course, in the original, the writer was not mentioned, just as was the case with the Gospel according to John. Even so, there is a definite connection between the Gospel and this epistle because of a similarity in content and style between the two writings. For instance, in the Gospel of John the author writes: "But these are written that ye may believe that Jesus is the Christ, the Son of God, and that believing ye might have life in his name" (20:31). And in the epistle we find this: "These things I have written to you that ye may know that ye have eternal life who believe on the name of the Son of God" (I John 5:13). So we find there is a connection between the fourth Gospel and this first epistle. It is commonly accepted, and I do not think there is any doubt now about it, that the one who wrote the Gospel is the one who wrote the letter, and we also believe that the one who wrote the Gospel as well as this letter is the apostle John.

John was among the first who followed the Lord Jesus. He was one of the disciples of John the Baptist, and one day while he and Andrew were with their master, Jesus passed by. John the Baptist said, "Behold the Lamb of God," and the two disciples left their master, followed the Lord Jesus, and stayed with Him that night. In the Gospel according to John Andrew's name was mentioned as one of the two disciples, but the other's name was not mentioned. However, we know that it was John himself. He was the one whom Jesus loved. He was the one who lay upon the breast of the Lord Jesus during the so-called Last Supper. He was the one who followed the Lord to the cross, the only one of the Twelve who was there when He was crucified. Among the twelve apostles he was the one who lived the longest. All the other eleven had died, but John lived almost to the close of the first century. So, we can say that his life spanned most of the first century.

A study of this man reveals that John was a most unusual person, because in him was a combination of temperaments which were truly opposite to each other. On the one hand, this apostle was a very reserved introvert. He was a deep thinker and one who was a contemplative who meditated a great deal. On the other hand, John possessed a fiery passion; and for this reason, the Lord Jesus bestowed upon him and his brother James the nickname: "the Sons of Thunder." These two opposing temperaments seem to have taken up residence in this man John; and under God's sovereign control and discipline, he was greatly used by the Lord.

Even though John did not write this letter to any particular church by name, we believe that because he had labored-during his last years-among the churches in the Roman provinces of Asia Minor (where Turkey is today), he had most likely addressed this first letter to those churches. Therefore, it would be helpful to know what was the condition of the early church at the close of the first century, since the apostle John wrote this letter during that time.

We know the church had its wonderful beginning on the day of Pentecost. When the Holy Spirit came down from heaven and one hundred and twenty believers were baptized into one body, that was the time the church formally came into being. It was such a glorious beginning! Within a generation, thirty years, the gospel was preached to the end of the world-from Jerusalem to all Judea and Samaria and even to Rome, because Rome at that time was considered the center as well as the end of the world. At the beginning, when God's people were together, they were in one accord, they loved one another, and they shared everything in common. That testimony was so strong that the Lord added to their number daily. That was the glorious beginning of the church.

Also at the beginning, the believers in Christ were opposed by the Jews and then by the Gentiles, and later on the Roman Empire persecuted the church. But at the time John wrote this epistle, evidently, there had occurred a lull in the Roman persecution of believers. It was now towards the end of the first century, and because of this, the Christians at that time were probably in the second or third generation. The glory of the new discovery of the gospel of Jesus Christ seemed to be gradually fading. The vision of the Lord Jesus seemed to grow dim, and because there was no persecution, people began to relax and their lives began to take on a more loose character. The enemy was able to use that kind of condition to creep into the church and thus, many false teachings commenced making their appearance.

If our understanding of Revelation chapters 2 and 3 is based on a prophetic approach, then we would describe the church at that time as having entered upon the Ephesian period. The first of the seven letters to the churches mentioned there is the letter to the church in Ephesus. What were the characteristics or features of that period in church history? Outwardly, everything continued on as usual. There was work, there was labor, there was endurance, knowledge and discernment. Everything seemed to go on as though nothing had changed; but the Lord said, "I am against you." Why? The explanation given them was that the believers had left their first love. Outwardly, everything seemed to be ordinary, nothing wrong, but the inner spring had vanished. They did not love God with all their hearts. Their love towards the Lord Jesus was now divided. They loved God but they also loved the world, and because of this, their love for one another had also weakened. They did not love one another to the extent of being willing to give their lives for each other. They became more self-centered than Christ-centered, and the Lord called them to repent, to remember from where they had fallen, to return and do the first work. That was the situation of the church at that time and to that kind of situation John addressed himself in this letter.

# LIVING FELLOWSHIP

This first letter of John is about Christian fellowship. First and foremost, the church (*ekklesia* in Greek) is a fellowship (*koinonia*): the *ekklesia* is the *koinonia*. The church, the called- out ones, whom God has called out from every tribe, tongue, nation and people, and has gathered together unto His name, becomes a fellowship. It is a living fellowship and is based upon the fellowship of the Father and the Son in the Spirit. Or we might word it another way: this fellowship of the believers is the extension of the fellowship of the Father and the Son in the Spirit. We know there is a fellowship between the Father and the Son, and the word *fellowship* itself means "sharing in common." In the Godhead there is perfect fellowship. The Father shares everything with the Son and the Son shares everything with the Father, and all such is done in the Spirit. The Father and the Son share everything in common-all the essence of the Godhead-and they are one.

In John chapter 17 we read that the Lord Jesus was addressing the Father in prayer, and He said this: "All that is mine is thine and all that is thine is mine" (v. 10). And later He said: "Thou, Father, art in Me and I in Thee" (v. 21). They share everything in common. All that is the Son's is the Father's and all that is the Father's is the Son's because they are one. One is in the other and the other is in the one. Their oneness is based on "in-ness." It is not an external thing but an inward reality; and because of this, their fellowship is perfect harmony and sweet communion. There is no shadow, no shade, no darkness. It is the fellowship in the entire universe.

We cannot imagine how joyful, how glorious that fellowship is between the Father and the Son. The Son always pleases the Father; the Father always finds His delight in the Son. That is the fellowship, the sharing in common, in the Godhead. But thank God, because of His great love, He desires to extend that fellowship to include mankind. Now we must remember that the fellowship the Father and the Son have with one another in the Spirit is something which no other person can ever demand or ask to join. We have no right to demand that we be accepted into that fellowship. We are completely unqualified and undeserving; but it is the good pleasure of the Father to extend that fellowship to mankind. "God is faithful, by whom ye have been called into the fellowship of his Son Jesus Christ our Lord" (I Corinthians 1:9).

We have no right whatsoever; nevertheless, we are called into the fellowship of God's Son, Jesus Christ our Lord. This fellowship of God's Son is that He is to share the Father with us. The Father is His exclusively from eternity. He is the only begotten Son and He is the only One who has the right to fellowship with the Father and to share with the Father everything in common. All that the Father has is the Son's and all that the Son has is the Father's; but thank God, today, He has called us into the fellowship of His Son. And the Son is willing to share His Father with us and all that the Father is. That is the reason why God can bless us with every spiritual blessing in the heavenlies in Christ Jesus. Our fellowship with the Father is through the Son, and as we fellowship with the Father we are likewise fellowshiping with the Son. It is to that unique fellowship we have been called.

Yet how did this fellowship come about? In order to extend Their fellowship to us the Persons of the Godhead had to do something. Fellowship is a very costly thing. It cost God the Father greatly, or to put it more plainly, it cost God His beloved and only Son in drawing us into Their fellowship. "For both he that sanctifies and those sanctified are all of one" (Hebrews 2:11).

He who sanctifies is the Lord; those sanctified are we, and we are all of one. How does that oneness come into being? He who sanctifies is the Son of God; those sanctified are fallen human beings. We in ourselves are certainly not one, but the Bible says, "He that sanctifies and those sanctified are all of one."

"Since therefore the children partake of blood and flesh, he also, in like manner, took part in the same, that through death he might annul him who has the might of death, that is, the devil; and might set free all those who through fear of death through the whole of their life were subject to bondage" (Hebrews 2:14-15).

We, His children, partake in blood and flesh. This English verb partake is *koinoneo* in Greek, that is, "sharing in common." We are born of flesh and blood, which is our common lot; but because we have flesh and blood, and are in bondage under sin, therefore, the Lord Jesus also, in like manner, took part in the same. In order to save us and draw us into being one with Him, He had to take upon himself flesh and blood. But that phrase, *took part in the same*, is not *koinoneo* (the verb form of koinonia); it is another Greek word, *metecho*. It means Christ Jesus took upon himself something which is outside of Him. He was not originally of flesh and blood as we are, but He deliberately took upon himself something which was outside of himself and it became His. He took part in flesh and blood. In His incarnation the Word became flesh. God the Father through His Son entered into flesh, and in His incarnation He identified himself with us who are flesh and blood. That was the first step.

The second step was that thus having been made a man, Jesus humbled himself and obeyed God; He died on the cross in our stead, taking upon himself all our sins so that we might be freed from death. Then, thirdly, in His resurrection the Lord Jesus released His own life to us; He gave His life to all who would believe in Him. In this manner, therefore, we are made one with Him. In other words, He identified himself with us at His incarnation and we are identified with Him in His death and resurrection. Christ's death is our death to the old creation, and His resurrection is our resurrection. We are raised into newness of life and are made one with Him. Let us realize that it cost God tremendously to bring us into the fellowship of His Son, and we can discern immediately that this fellowship which we are drawn into is not some outward thing; it is an inward reality; it is a matter of life. This fellowship is based upon the life which He has given to each one of us; and hence, we are now in that unique fellowship of the Son with the Father.

# PRINCIPLES OF FELLOWSHIP

What is fellowship? Fellowship is based on life and is the sharing of life. Anything which is not life, which is not the sharing of Christ, cannot be considered as fellowship. Today, we too often think of fellowship as something outward. Just as many people today think of the church as an outward organization. But the church is the called-out ones gathered together to be a living fellowship, to share the life of Christ, to manifest Him together.

Sometimes we say, "Well, let's have some fellowship together." What do we do? We share our problems. Is that fellowship? The more you fellowship in this way, the more depressed you become. Worse than that, sometimes we gather together for fellowship and we talk about politics, social problems, and all such things. Is that fellowship? That is social interaction. Or we try to teach each other the teachings and the doctrines about the Lord Jesus and about all the different interpretations concerning the truth. Is that fellowship? It can be, if *Christ* is being shared; but too often it is only a matter of mind to mind being shared. Now, we may have a very clever, analytical and penetrating mind, and we may think we see something in the Bible which other people have not seen and so we share it. We share our mind with other people, but where is Christ? After we have shared such with others, their knowledge may be increased but their life has not been increased an inch. Can we call that fellowship?

Fellowship is the sharing of Christ, the sharing of His life. Anything that is not of life is not fellowship. Because of this, we realize how much fellowship we must have with the Father and with the Son! In other words, our fellowship with one another is measured proportionally by our fellowship which we have with the Father and with the Son. We cannot have interrupted fellowship with the Father and with the Son and expect to have uninterrupted fellowship with our brothers and sisters. That is impossible. Hence, the degree of our fellowship in sharing with our brothers and sisters is determined by the degree-by the depths with which-we have fellowship with the Father and with the Son. How much we have known and experienced of the Father and of the Son will determine the extent of our fellowship with our brothers and sisters, and no more. Thus, we shall discover that fellowship is a very disciplined matter.

Let me repeat: *koinonia, fellowship, a sharing in common* can only occur because we have something in common, and that something is the life of Christ. Therefore, when we fellowship, we fellowship in life; and because of this, this fellowship is all- inclusive among God's people. All who have the life of Jesus Christ are in that fellowship. Now, today, we may refer to this fellowship or that fellowship, but such is unscriptural since there is only one fellowship. It is the fellowship between the Father and the Son in the Spirit; it is the fellowship of God's Son, Jesus Christ the Lord; it is the fellowship of the apostles. "They continued in the teaching and the fellowship of the apostles" (Acts 2:42). The fellowship of the apostles is the fellowship of God's Son, Jesus Christ. So the fellowship of the apostles, as it is extended to us, is the sharing of Christ with us. It is the one fellowship in the universe, and there is none other; and because of this, it has its practical application. In other words, we who know the Lord must receive all who have the life of the Lord Jesus. We cannot be exclusive. If we exclude anyone who has the life of the Lord Jesus, we become a sect, a party, a division. And it displeases the Lord because this fellowship of His is all- inclusive; it includes all who know the Father and the Son, all who have the life of God in Christ Jesus.

On the other hand, this fellowship is extremely exclusive. Everything and anyone that does not have life, and no matter how good the thing or the person is, cannot be in the fellowship. We cannot draw certain people into the fellowship because they are very good, are very moral, have a good social standing or have a good name in the world. No; we cannot do that because this fellowship is based on life. Even Nicodemus had to be born again in order to belong to that fellowship. Thank God, we have been born again into this fellowship. There is no way to join it but to be born into it. The membership book for this fellowship is not on earth. We cannot find that book anywhere, not even in a safe. The book of life is in heaven, and that is where our membership is. All who believe in the Lord Jesus, all who have the

Son, have eternal life, and they belong to this fellowship. We all have something in common. God has shared with us His beloved Son, His own life, and so we have fellowship with the Father, with the Son, and with one another.

Then, too, fellowship is not based on light but on life. By light is meant here that there may be some light which you have concerning the word of God. We believe all the word of God, but there are so many different interpretations. Some people say they have light on a certain portion of Scripture, and other people think they have a different light on that same portion of Scripture. Among God's people there are those, as it were, who have different light. I do not know whether it is light or darkness, but they profess they have light on God's word; yet because of their different interpretations, they divide God's people. Their attitude is: "If you do not believe in my interpretation on a certain portion of the Scriptures, you are out." Let us be reminded that even though you and I may have different light, different interpretations on the Scriptures, if you and I have the same Christ, we must have fellowship with one another. None of such differences should affect our fellowship, because church fellowship is based on life. Thank God, it is not based on light, it is not based on how much you or I know about the Scriptures, or how you or I know it; it is based upon the life of Christ which both you and I have received by grace through faith. Then we have fellowship with one another.

## JOHN'S REPORT

The apostle John begins his letter with this matter of fellowship. "That which was from the beginning, that which we have heard, which we have seen with our eyes; that which we contemplated, and our hands handled, concerning the word of life" (I John 1:1).

Fellowship is very personal; it is experiential in nature because you cannot share or report to others what you have not seen or heard. Accordingly, fellowship is based upon what you have seen and what you have heard. Therefore, you can report and share it with others; and when you share it they will see what you see and hear what you hear. That is the joy of fellowship.

"That which was from the beginning ..." Who or what is that which was from the beginning? The Word. "In the beginning was the Word and the Word was with God and the Word was God" (John 1:1). John is trying to share with us Jesus, the Word of life. He is the beginning; He is from the beginning; He is God eternal.

"That which we have heard ..." Where did we hear? We heard from the prophets of old. That which was from the beginning was unknown, but God has spoken through the prophets to our fathers in pieces and fragments, in many parts and in many ways (see Hebrews 1:1). "That which we have seen with our eyes ..." when the Word became flesh and dwelt among us. "That which we contemplated ..." The word *contemplated* means "gazed upon." You gaze upon Him until you see something which other people do not see; in other words, there is a revelation. "The Word became flesh and tabernacled among men and we have contemplated or gazed upon Him and have seen the glory of Him as the glory of the Son with the Father" (see John 1:14). In other words, as you contemplate, the Spirit of God reveals what He really is to you. Hence, we learn here that the disciples have received revelation about this man Jesus. Next: "and our hands handled ..." When? After the resurrection of the Lord Jesus, the Lord told Thomas, "Touch Me. Put your finger into My wounded hand and feel that there is a hole there. You can handle Me" (see John 20:27). Resurrection.

Hence, here in summary is the entire history of the gospel story-His story: the Son of God becoming Man; how He then died for us; how He next was raised from the dead; how He is the Word of eternal life; how this life has been manifested in the flesh-in the Person of the Lord Jesus; how we who have followed Him have seen and borne witness to Him and now report to you this eternal life. This is life. Eternal life is not something outside of God; this life is not only something which God gives. Eternal life is God himself in the Person of His Son. He is the true God; He is the eternal life. This eternal life is more than simply a matter of living in endless time; eternal life is the first quality of living. And God in His Son is the eternal life.

"This eternal life," writes the apostle John, "we have seen and heard." Jesus' disciples had personal experience of this eternal life and, therefore, they report this to us, which means they share it with us. And as they share it with us we obtain it as well; we also receive eternal life; for we, too, now see and hear the Word of life. Then the apostle said this: "Let me tell you what this fellowship is. We are reporting this to you so that you may have fellowship with us. We are sharing with you what we have gained in order that you may have this in common with us; but do understand that what we share with you has its root somewhere else. Its root is verily with the Father and with the Son. We are not fellowshiping and sharing with you of ourselves. No. Peter, for example, is not fellowshiping or sharing himself with you; on the contrary, he is sharing the Christ who is in him with you. Our fellowship is with the Father and with the Son, and as you receive this fellowship-as you are drawn into this fellowship with us-you shall enter into the fellowship which is with the Father and with the Son."

"These things write we to you that your joy may be full." There is nothing which can bring us more joy than real spiritual fellowship. Through fellowship with your brothers and sisters, you are actually fellowshiping in the spirit with the Father and the Son. Can you find anything more full of joy than that fellowship? As you fellowship with your brothers and sisters, you are in reality fellowshiping Christ; and as you are fellowshiping Christ, you are fellowshiping with your brothers and sisters. How full must be this joy! Fellowship is heaven on earth.

# PRACTICE OF FELLOWSHIP

Now, having laid down the principles of fellowship, let us next discuss the practice of it. As we have said, fellowship is based on life; therefore, when we practice fellowship, it has to be practiced in accordance with life. I think that is evident. We cannot practice fellowship outside of the nature of life, eternal life. This eternal life which we receive has its nature and its character; and it is only as we develop our fellowship according to life's character and nature will our fellowship increase. But if in any way we violate the nature of that life, then we will suffer and our fellowship will be hindered. And that is what I John is all about.

The church towards the close of the first century had begun to lose her first love because of her dimmed vision of Christ. Therefore, the believers' fellowship among themselves had been weakened to the point that it was often interrupted, hindered or damaged. So John tried to help them to see how their fellowship could be spiritually revitalized and increased.

By its very nature, true Christian fellowship is living. Anything which lives will grow. When it stops growing, that is a sign that the process of death has begun. Fellowship is the same thing. Christian fellowship is a growing process. We do not come to a point in its process wherein we can say, "Now we have arrived; we cannot grow anymore." To think or to utter this is death. The fellowship between the Father and the Son is ever growing and never ending; and our fellowship together is the same. Is that not wonderful?

# GOD IS LIGHT (I JOHN 1:5-2:28)

In I John the character or the nature of God is defined or described by three different statements: 1. God is light 2. God is righteous 3. God is love. Let us take up each of these in that order. "This is the message which we have heard from him, and declare to you, that God is light, and in him is no darkness at all" (I John 1:5). Here it says, "God is light." The light in view here is different from the light which I mentioned earlier. That light discussed earlier had to do with the interpretation of the Scriptures. Of course, God's word is the lamp at our feet; it is the light for our steps (see Psalm 119:105). The word of God is light, but we are not talking about that because we are talking here about fellowship. Fellowship is not based upon what light you or I may have on the word of God in terms of interpretation. Fellowship is upon light, but what light? God is light. There is therefore a great difference here. God himself is light. That is His nature, His character. He is pure, brilliant, glorious, with no darkness nor shadow nor shade, and no change, He is full light. That is God himself. "In Him was life, and the life was the light of men" (John 1:4). In Christ is life; in the Son is life, and that life is the light of man. In chapter 8 of the Gospel of John, Jesus is quoted as saying: "I am the light of the world. He that follows me shall not walk in darkness, but shall have the light of life."

The life we receive is Christ, and this life has the nature of light. In other words, the life that we have in Christ is to be our light; for He is the light of life. This light in us will shine, and as it shines, we walk forward. We cannot walk in darkness because we will stumble. As Christians we do not walk by outside rules or regulations; we walk instead by the light of life in us. As we follow the Lord the light in us will blink, will shine, and will reveal one step ahead of us. The light of life will not give us the light for our whole life's journey, but it will provide us light for our next step. If we obey the light of life, then we can walk with the Lord. We go a step, and then the light of life will shine another step before us. That is Christian growth.

"If we walk in the light ..." The word if here in this passage is not meant to be saying that we may or we may not. "If we walk in the light ..." We, as believers, must walk in the light. Where is the light? Again I say, the light is not the interpretations of God's word, because there are too many different interpretations. The light is the light of life-we follow life. Put it another way: for him who walks according to the Spirit it is life and peace (see Romans 8). In other words, if we follow the light in us as it shines upon our path and we obey it, then God is in the light. Now, of course, there is a huge difference here between ourselves and God as it pertains to light. We walk in the light; yet God is not only in the light but He himself is also the light. God lives in the impenetrable light and His light is full, perfect, a hundred percent. God is holy, pure, glorious. But we walk in the light of life as it shines on our path, and if we do, then the wonderful thing is, we have fellowship with God.

There is no fellowship between light and darkness (see II Corinthians 6:14). We may therefore ask how God, who is light and in whom there is no darkness, can fellowship with us, who, even though we have the light of life in us, have so much darkness around us and in us? The answer is that this is God's mercy and grace upon us. God is in the light, and He is light. We have the light of life in us and God says, "Now walk." As His light shines forth one step on our path, we walk out that step. So far as our experience is concerned, even though the difference is unspeakable and insurmountable between the extent of our light and that of God who is light, nevertheless, the quality or the nature of the light is the same. And hence, God can say to us: "As long as you walk in the light I will have fellowship with you." Even though we still have much darkness in us, that will not interfere with the fellowship between us and God because we have obeyed the light of life which we have today. Is that not an evidence of God's marvelous grace? On the other hand, if we do not walk in the light of life which has been given us, then we walk in darkness and there can be no fellowship between us and God until we confess our sins. In order that our fellowship with God the Father and with the Son remains uninterrupted, it is extremely important and most fundamental that every believer learns to walk faithfully in the light of life that is given him or her.

Of course, there will be a great difference in our experience, one from another. Some people are like little children in whom the life is still young, so the light shines only a little. But as long as you obey that light, you are all right; your fellowship with God is not interrupted. Then you grow to be young people. As your life grows, your light grows; and if you obey that, then you have fellowship with God. Then you grow to be fathers, and the light grows much brighter; and you need to obey. If you do not, you are in darkness and your fellowship will be interrupted. In other words, this fellowship with the Father is a living one; and that is the reason why you and I cannot judge one another. You cannot use your standard and put it upon another brother or sister because he or she may at that moment be a child in the faith and, according to him or her, he or she has obeyed. But you may be a young person or a father in the faith who knows more, and has received more of God's light, so you need to be more faithful. If you are not, you are worse than a child.

"If we walk in the light as He is in the light, we have fellowship with one another." The strange thing here is, this particular *one another* is not between us and the Father and the Son; strictly speaking, it refers to our fellowship with our fellow believers. If we walk in the light as He is in the light, we have fellowship with the Father and with the Son, and it is because of this that we have fellowship with one another. If we do not walk in the light, our fellowship with the Father and the Son is not right, and therefore we can have no fellowship with our brothers and sisters. I think this is clear.

"And the blood of Jesus Christ His Son cleanses us from all sin." Think of that! As you fellowship with your brothers and sisters, as you exchange light and life, the light grows. Perhaps I am one candlelight, and as I fellowship with my brother, he serves as another candlelight. Immediately, there are now two candlelights and the light grows. As the light grows, you realize your darkness that has never been exposed before. And thank God, the blood of God's Son Jesus Christ cleanses us from all sin, and so we increase in life. Is that not true? When you fellowship with your brothers and sisters and nothing happens, something is wrong with that fellowship. If you truly fellowship with your brothers and sisters, are you not convicted? Oftentimes, when you fellowship with brothers and sisters you are convicted because the light of life in him or her begins to shine upon you and in that particular area in your life you are in darkness. But then you begin to see; therefore, you confess and the blood of Jesus cleanses you, and your character is thus purified. This is the glory of fellowship.

Let us not think that fellowship is cheap and that it is nothing more than having a good time. No; sometimes, fellowship can be very costly; because if you dare to truly fellowship with your brothers and sisters, you will open yourself to being exposed, but also to being delivered. Do you dare to fellowship with God? Let us not think fellowship with God is all roses. There are many thorns there, numerous purgings, frequent emptyings, and many works to be done; but thank God, nothing is more glorious than what fellowship can give.

# GOD IS RIGHTEOUS (I JOHN 2:29-4:6)

We have seen that fellowship is based on life, the life given to us in Christ Jesus. Fellowship has its origin in the fellowship of the Godhead, and this fellowship between the Father and the Son in the Spirit has been extended to us through Christ the Son. The degree or extent of our fellowship with one another is determined by the degree or extent of our fellowship with the Father and with the Son. In order to have our fellowship increased without hindrance we must learn to develop along the nature of God's life in us. First, God is light, so we must walk in the light of life in order to have fellowship and to grow from little children to young men to fathers. Next, we see that God is righteous (see I John 2:29). Whatever God does is righteous because He is righteous in His very character. It is not a matter of some righteous acts which God does, but it is a being righteous in himself. God cannot deny himself. That is, He will not and cannot do anything other than what is just and right.

Now we are the children of God. "See what love the Father has given to us" (I John 3:1). As children of God, we have His seed-that is, His life-in us (see I John 3:9). The life in us is a righteous life. This distinguishes us from the world-from the children of the devil (see I John 3:10). The latter sin, and cannot but practice sin, for this is the nature of their father. We as children of God, however, do not practice sin, for sin is lawlessness, that is, it is against the law of God (see I John 3:4). As children of God, we should not sin for that would be against the nature of the life in us, that would be unlike God. And we may not sin, because this life given to us is a righteous and sinless life: Christ was tempted in all things, but without sinning; for His life overcame all temptation and thus, He did no sin. Nevertheless, it is also true that we still have the possibility of sinning-sinning against our new nature-because we still have the flesh in us. However, we do not *practice* sin, that is to say, we do not "commit sin" as a habit (see I John 3:8-9 AV) nor do we "keep on sinning" nor "continue to sin" (both in I John 3:6 NIV). Instead of practicing sin, we practice righteousness, for God is righteous. The righteousness in view here is practical righteousness, not the righteousness of God which comes to us when we believe in the Lord Jesus Christ nor Christ our righteousness as the robe with which we are clothed. No, these give us acceptance and access to God. The righteousness in view here is the righteous acts of the saints (see Revelation 19:8: "it was given to her that she should be clothed with fine linen, bright and pure: for this fine linen is the righteousnesses of the saints"): we do the things which are right in the sight of God, such as loving the brethren: we do what Christ has done: He loved us and has laid down His life for us, so we too ought to lay down our lives for the brethren (see I John 3:16).

We often are concerned with not sinning, which we should; but we neglect the positive aspect of practicing righteousness. Many of God's children are careless in living a righteous life. They consider righteousness as a thing of the past, that is, they have become righteous in Christ, and that is good enough. They fail to see that God requires us to practice righteousness. This is one of the errors which John fights against. False and wrong teaching leads to loose and sinful living. If we do not practice righteousness, how can we prove that we are God's children? How can we fellowship with God and fellowship with one another? "For what participation is there between righteousness and lawlessness?" (II Corinthians 6:14)

How do we know we are doing the right thing? "And hereby we shall know that we are of the truth, and shall persuade our hearts before him-that if our hearts condemn us, God is greater than our hearts and knows all things" (I John 3:19-20). We know we do the right thing or not because God has given us a conscience of the heart purified by the blood of the Lord Jesus. A purified conscience is most important to have in our daily walk. For God is able to speak to us through our conscience. If our conscience condemns us, we know that God has condemned us because His heart is greater than ours and He knows all things. But if our conscience does not condemn us, we have boldness towards God because we have kept His commandments and have practiced the things pleasing in His sight (see I John 3:21-22). Our hearts are of course smaller than God's; our consciences condemn us far less than what God condemns.

So, then, how is it possible that if our hearts do not condemn us, we have boldness towards God? We not only can fellowship with God, but even have the confidence that He will hear our prayers. This again shows the condescending love of God. He is willing to fellowship with us so long as our consciences are clear before Him. This is the way to lead us on to more maturity. Our consciences will tell us that we must owe nothing to anyone except love (see Romans 13:8). We must love in deed and in truth (see I John 3:18), otherwise our hearts will condemn us. The reason why our hearts serve as a measure in fellowship is because God has given us His Spirit (see I John 3:24). The Spirit of God is the Spirit of the incarnate Son. He is concerned with our daily walk because the Son of God came in the flesh and also walked on earth in righteousness. Any spirit who does not confess that Jesus Christ came in the flesh is not of God but is of the antichrist (see I John 4:3). Such erroneous teaching corrupts righteous living. This is the spirit of the world, but He who is in us is greater than he who is in the world. Hence, we are able to overcome (see I John 4:4).

So, if we want to fellowship with God, we must keep our consciences void of offense. When the consciences of our hearts condemn us, we are unable to come to God. We know we are not what He is, therefore we are afraid to come. Thank God, the blood is always available. We must not allow the accuser of the brethren to take advantage of our unrighteous condition; rather, the brethren overcame him by the blood of the Lamb (see Revelation 12:11).

The same is it with respect to our fellowship with one another: if we have anything against our brother, or if we do not forgive concerning whatever our brother sins against us in; our fellowship with one another is hindered until reconciliation is made and forgiveness is given. This is why the Lord says, "If therefore thou shouldest offer thy gift at the altar, and there shouldest remember that thy brother has something against thee, leave there thy gift before the altar, and first go, be reconciled to thy brother, and then come and offer thy gift" (Matthew 5:23-24). Whether we practice righteousness or not affects our fellowship with God.

# GOD IS LOVE (I JOHN 4:7-5:12)

Fellowship is according to life, yet not our old life, but the new life of Christ given to us by God. Now the character or nature of this new life is love, for God is love. The love of God is more than an emotion, it is the very nature of God. He loves not because He is emotionally stirred by external circumstances but because love is what He is. This is a basic difference between God's love and our so-called love. Our love is emotionally based, since it is conditioned by external circumstances. It is basically selfish. It is quite limited in scope and duration. But the love of God is an inward character. It is active and spontaneous. It is self-sacrificing, and it knows no limit.

We are called into this fellowship of love. First, we are to see and experience God's love towards us; and, then, we are to love one another as He has loved us. What kind of love is this love of God which draws us into this fellowship? (1) It is a love which comes forth naturally; for God is love: He cannot help but love. There is no second thought or consideration in His love, He just loves. (2) It is a love that was manifested through God sending His beloved Son into the world that we might live through Him. It is therefore a practical love, a sacrificial love, a selfless love. God thinks of us and counts not the cost. (3) God loves us first, that is to say, His love is not a reaction but an action. His love is not governed by our love towards Him. By loving us first He opens the way of fellowship to us.

Having received such love from God, we ought to love one another with the same love. By loving one another, we manifest and prove our love to God. By loving those who are begotten of God, we show our love to Him who has begotten us. How can we say we love God yet we do not love our brethren? If we cannot show love to these whom we see, how can we prove we love God whom we do not see? (see I John 4:20) Our fellowship with one another is dependent on our abiding in God. It is the outcome and overflow of our connection with Him. The more we abide in God, the more He abides in us. Thus, His love begins to flow from us to the brethren.

A passage of Scripture in I John mentions "perfect love" (4:18). What is perfect love? It does not mean perfection in the sense that there is absolutely nothing which can be improved upon. Only God's love is perfect. In relation to us, perfect love is a love that is perfected by our abiding in God's love. "Abiding" means "making our home in." It is not an erratic experience but a permanent condition. As we abide in God's love we abide in Him, and He in us. We have fellowship with God and we have boldness in the day of judgment, knowing that we have done what He has done. Such love casts out all fear. We love God with all our hearts. We love because He has first loved us.

Let us move forward in this matter of fellowship in accordance with the nature of life. God is light; so we walk in the light. God is righteous; so we practice righteousness. God is love; and hence we love one another, and as we do so, fellowship increases. May the Lord bless us.

*Let us pray:*

Dear heavenly Father, what can we say? We have no right, we do not deserve anything; yet Thou dost extend Thy wonderful, glorious fellowship to us. Thou dost share Thy Son with us and Thy Son shares Thee with us. Oh, we do praise and thank Thee that today we are called into the fellowship of God's Son, Jesus Christ. Our fellowship is with the Father and with the Son and with one another. Father, we do pray that we may truly understand what this fellowship is, that we may treasure it, that we may be willing to pay any cost for it. And we do pray that our fellowship may increase and grow so that Thou mayest be glorified and our joy may be full. We ask in the name of our Lord Jesus. Amen.

www.ingramcontent.com/pod-product-compliance
Lightning Source LLC
LaVergne TN
LVHW040941150826
845672LV00008B/2482

* 9 7 9 8 5 3 3 9 9 1 6 7 4 *